NO MORE TEARS

HOPE FOR THOSE WHO HAVE LOST

BILL HATHAWAY

No More Tears

"And God Shall Wipe Away all Tears"
Rev. 21:4

The contents of this book are the result the Lord's leading the author of over 55 years of preaching the Gospel on two continents to write a book designed to help, encourage and comfort those who have lost their life's companion and dearest friend on earth. It's one thing to be the minister officiating at the funeral service of one who has lost a spouse, and being the one ministered to.

Following the "Home going" of my dear wife, the Lord has led me to start the Precious Memories Support Ministry for the sole purpose of encouraging others. My sole desire and prayer to God is that this book will be a blessing to you. The messages in this book come from one who has personally experienced this deepest valley of life. It is my desire that Precious Memories Support Ministry chapters be started in cities across the United States and around the world. In addition to being a blessing to those who have lost a spouse, these messages can be used as devotions at Precious Memories Support Ministry meetings.

Cover Design: Keith Locke
Book Design: Zach Dyer

ISBN: 978-0-9817769-3-4

Dr. Bill Hathaway
3149 N. Maranatha Ln. #8
Springfield, Missouri 65803

21stCENTURY
PRESS
READING YOU LOUD AND CLEAR

Preface

It gives me much pleasure to write this preface to Bill Hathaway's timely book "No More Tears." Such a book has been long overdue and meets a great need.

I am also honored to be asked to write this preface. Bill and I have a close tie working together for our Lord over three decades on what many say is the most difficult mission field. Bill has been one of our most effective missionaries in Japan. He is fluent in the language and a successful church planter. He and Dixie are dearly loved in Japan.

I can relate to what Bill is writing in this book because we both have come down the path of precious memories together. My first wife Evelyn, graduated to glory in 1989 also leaving a long trail of precious memories. These memories live on in the hearts and lives of the people to whom the Lord has sent us to minister.

The focal point of this book is that it pays to serve the Lord. And lives spent serving the Lord loads our hearts with a comfort for the lonely hours after our spouses have been called home to glory.

I sincerely pray the impact of this book will also result in many surrendering their lives to follow in the footsteps of Bill and Dixie Hathaway to the mission field!

Lookin' up, Pressin' on,

Dr. Lavern F. Rodgers
Baptist Bible Fellowship International
Missionary to Japan since 1949

"Encouragement is the transfer of strength."

Frank Moseley
President of SOS

Dedication

I would like to express my appreciation for the encouragement and advice as I wrote the pages of this very needed and helpful book, designed to give comfort and advice to those who have lost their dearest friend, their life's mate.

Among others are the following:

Pastor Mark Rounsaville, Baptist Temple of Springfield

Frank Moseley, President & Founder of
The SOS Soulwinning Ministry

Dr. Ray Melugin, Pastor & Evangelist

Phil Melugin, President & Owner of
Integrity Home Care, Springfield, MO

Community Hospices of America, Springfield, MO

Dr. Bill Dowell Jr., Academic Dean of BBC, Springfield, MO

Dr. Keith Bassham, Baptist Bible Tribune Editor

Pastor Steve Day, Friendship Baptist Church, Wichita, KS.

Joe Levanti, Founder of Horseshoe Theatre, Mt. Vernon, MO

Many Pastors and Missionaries from around the world

Dr. C. S. Lovett, President of Personal Christianity

Rev. Vernon Longstaff, Pastor and personal friend

Dr. Lavern Rodgers, Missionary to Japan

My Family: Ike, Paul, Jim and Ruth & their families

Rev. George Bryant, Bryant Ministries

Mrs. Ruth Bryant, who proof-read this book

Ike Foster, Missionary to Korea

Gary Longstaff, General Manager of KWFC

Table of Contents

Part One

Part Two

Poems

Appendix

Prologue
How the Precious Memories Support Ministry Began

Ministries are usually born out of a need or are the outcome of some experience or valley that someone has gone through. Such is the case with Precious Memories. Dixie and I were married for just over 51 years when she was told she had a fast moving cancer and not even chemo would help. Just seventeen days after we were notified of her cancer, at precisely 6:45 PM, February 4, 2005, Dixie quietly slipped out of her physical body and was ushered by the angels into the presence of her Savior Whom she loved and served for so many years.

Having been a missionary and pastor for over 50 years, I have officiated at countless funerals. I have stood by the casket of a husband or wife and tried to render consolation and comfort. I thought I understood what the person was going through, but now I know. Without a doubt, losing a spouse is one of the deepest, darkest and longest valleys of life. Nothing can compare with it. Many have told me, "I can't imagine," or "I've never experienced what you have, so I just don't know what to say." I don't have to say that. I know what a person goes through when their spouse is gone.

Thus the need for Precious Memories was born. The Lord impressed my heart to start the Precious Memories Support Ministry. Believing that it is almost impossible to go through this valley without the Lord, I asked the Pastor of Baptist Temple of Springfield, Missouri if we could start one in the church. He enthusiastically offered a room in the church for the meeting. Since then interest has been shown for Precious Memories Support Ministries to be started in other cities, states and foreign countries.

There are other support groups for the purpose of encouraging and comforting the bereaved. Most of these groups are for those grieving the loss of any loved one: mother, father, son, daughter and any other relative or very close friend. I am deeply grateful for the help I have received from Integrity Home Care in Springfield and the Community Hospices of America in Springfield, Missouri. Both of these wonderful organizations work with Precious Memories by referring people to us for help. Some hospitals also have such a program. However, Precious Memories is a Christian-centered organization that is open to anyone in need of the comfort, encouragement and guidance of others who know what they are experiencing. Some attend our meetings who do not claim to be Christians. Precious Memories is for them as well as for Christians. Everyone is invited and urged to come. Interaction with those who have traveled the road you are traveling can help you.

Perhaps your spouse has been gone for several years and you feel you do not need the help we can offer. With your experience, you can be a source of strength to those just entering this valley. No one understands the need more than people like you who have traveled this lonely road. May God bless you and comfort you who are experiencing the loneliness of sorrow.

Part One

These one-page messages gained from personal experience and from others who have lost a spouse are meant to encourage, strengthen and comfort those who have lost a spouse.

Although these messages apply in a special way to those who have lost a spouse, most of them can apply to anyone who has experienced the loss of any loved one, be it a mother or dad, child, brother, sister, any close relative or friend.

There Is Hope

Everything has changed. Nothing is the same. You are all alone. You constantly say, "It's just not real." "I know she/he is gone, but it's just not real." Without a doubt this is the most heart-wrenching experience you have ever known. Without warning something will trigger the emotions of your heart and you will break down and cry, sometimes uncontrollably. You breathe so deeply that you may feel that it seems that you will die from that agony that comes from inside your chest. You wonder how long this sorrow will last. You don't like to eat alone and yet, sometimes it isn't easy when you are with friends. Can you relate to any or all of these feelings? Well, I want to tell you from experience... there is hope.

If you have had a personal encounter with the Lord and have trusted Him as your Lord and Savior, He has made a promise to you. "Let your conversation be without covetousness; and be content with such things as ye have: for he hath said, I will never leave thee, nor forsake thee" (Heb. 13:5). That's a promise. You are not alone. Oh, I know you may feel alone, but you can trust the Word of God. Therefore, I want to tell you, from experience...and from the Word of God...there is hope.

The hope that comes from above is both real and comforting. There is also hope and comfort that comes from those who know from experience the valley you are crossing. The Word of God says, "Who comforteth us in all our tribulation, that we may be able to comfort them which are in any trouble, by the comfort wherewith we ourselves are comforted of God" (2 Cor. 1:4). My prayer is that you will find a Precious Memories Support group near you. They are there for you and ready to render the support you need...there is hope.

NOTE: There are materials available to help start a Precious Memories Support Ministry for your church. Contact Baptist Temple of Springfield, Missouri located at 2655 N Grant Ave., Springfield, MO 65803. Telephone 417-831-2631.

Do You Really Know What I am Experiencing?

Just after Dixie went to her reward, a young man said to me, "I understand what you are going through." But did he? Most people said, "I just can't imagine." That's really all that most people can say. No one knows what a person experiences when a person's life mate is suddenly gone. It's impossible to know. I tell people, "I hope you never have to experience this." One man told me, "I don't know what to say. I would just be putting my foot in my mouth and saying the wrong thing."

Well, in this small book I want to be a source of encouragement and comfort to you. I have not only experienced first-hand the "valley of the shadow of death," but I have made an intense study of how to help and encourage others. I know what you are experiencing. Everyone handles grief differently. I believe it's different for a man or woman. It's different depending on how long one has been married. It's different for those who are older compared with younger people. It's different if you have the support of others and if you don't have support. Some are by nature more emotional than others. There are many variables. So all of what I say here may or may not apply to you. I am positive that most of it will apply and be a source of help, comfort and encouragement.

You don't have to travel this valley alone. First and most important...you need to remember that Jesus promised never to leave you (Heb. 13:5). Then there are those who are going through what you are experiencing right now. They need your help and you need theirs. That's what Precious Memories is all about. I pray that you will find one near you.

When it First Happens

For some, it is sudden; no warning. The doctor comes to her bedside with the news, "I'm sorry, you have cancer and it's gone too far. There is nothing we can do." Within a few days, she is gone. Or maybe it was an accident caused by a drunk driver. Or perhaps it happened following many weeks or months of suffering. No matter when it happens, it is always sudden!

During the funeral you are in a daze. "Is this really happening?" you ask yourself. "It can't be." Your family and friends come to your rescue. They are there for you during the funeral and for a few weeks. Then you're all alone. The funeral is over. Your family is gone and your friends seem to have forgotten. But you haven't! For you, the long night has just begun.

You may experience anger…at God and even perhaps at your departed loved one. Or maybe you are going through the stage of non-acceptance. "I just can't believe it happened."

Let me help you. I've been there. I know what you are going through. At this time, I know it's hard to believe, but remember Romans 8:28 is still true. "And we know that all things work together for good to them that love God, to them who are the called according to his purpose." You know that is true, but the reality of what has happened is so overwhelming that you doubt.

God still loves you. He is with you. Hebrews 13:5 states, "Let your conversation be without covetousness; and be content with such things as ye have: for he hath said, I will never leave thee, nor forsake thee." Count on that!

The loving arms of Jesus are open to receive you into His bosom and to give you the comfort you need in this most devastating valley of life. "Come unto me, all ye that labour and are heavy laden, and I will give you rest" (Matt. 11:28).

When Will I Get Over It?

No! No! No! That's the wrong question to ask. Most people never "get over it" and you shouldn't want to "get over it." If you've been with your spouse for any length of time, there are many Precious Memories that you should cherish the rest of your life. So if you feel you are still having a hard time, don't be concerned about that. Everyone is different. Some go through the funeral and the first few months like a soldier, but grief cannot be ignored. The Bible is full of examples of those who grieved over the loss of their loved one. Even Jesus grieved the loss of His friend Lazarus. "Jesus wept" (John 11:35). Here's a scripture I like. "…weeping may endure for a night, but joy cometh in the morning" (Psa. 30:5). Weeping is both natural and healthy. There is coming a day when the Lord will wipe away all tears. "And God shall wipe away all tears from their eyes; and there shall be no more death, neither sorrow, nor crying, neither shall there be any more pain: for the former things are passed away" (Rev. 21:4).

Jeremiah was a man of sorrows. Listen to what he said. "Woe is me for my hurt! my wound is grievous: but I said, Truly this is a grief, and I must bear it" (Jer. 10:19). Your "hurt" is truly grievous, but you can "bear it." Remember this, "There hath no temptation taken you but such as is common to man: but God is faithful, who will not suffer you to be tempted above that ye are able; but will with the temptation also make a way to escape, that ye may be able to bear it" (1 Cor. 10:13). Don't be afraid to grieve, even in front of others. God gave us emotions; and grieving, sorrow and tears are a gift of God. Don't try to "get over it;" rather, allow yourself to feel it. If you had no tears, what would God have to wipe away?

> *"For thou hast delivered my soul from death, mine eyes from tears, and my feet from falling" (Psa. 116:8).*

> *"They that sow in tears shall reap in joy" (Psa. 126:5).*

The "Why" Question

Without a doubt the question of "Why?" is the most asked question concerning death. The Bible is full of "Why's." David asked, "Why standest thou afar off, O Lord? Why hidest thou thyself in times of trouble" (Psa. 10:1)? And again in Psalm 88:14, "Lord, why castest thou off my soul? Why hidest thou thy face from me?" I am not able to answer all the "why" questions, but let me give you a few thoughts from God's Word.

◆ *God does all things for our good.* The Bible says, "Trust in the LORD with all thine heart; and lean not unto thine own understanding" (Prov. 3:5). I don't understand a lot of things, but I trust God and I cling to Romans 8:28.

◆ *Everyone must die sometime, ready or not!* "And as it is appointed unto men once to die, but after this the judgment" (Heb. 9:27). Everyone must die, but it seems we are never ready to deal with it.

◆ *Because of sin, people die.* "Wherefore, as by one man sin entered into the world, and death by sin; and so death passed upon all men, for that all have sinned" (Rom. 5:12). Remember however, in heaven there is no sin and therefore no more death. "...Death is swallowed up in victory" (1 Cor. 15:54).

◆ *God's timing is always right.* "My times are in thy hand..." (Psa. 31:15). God has everything under control and He is never in a hurry. The question of "why now?" will be forgotten when we are united in heaven.

◆ *Our present suffering and sorrows cannot be compared with heaven.* "For I reckon that the sufferings of this present time are not worthy to be compared with the glory which shall be revealed in us" (Rom. 8:18).

Conclusion: Remember this, according to Hebrews 13:5, you have a Friend who is always with you.

In Light of Romans 8:28, What Good Can Come from My Loss?

Jesus told His disciples, "Blessed are they that mourn: for they shall be comforted" (Mat. 5:4). You mean that people who mourn are "blessed"? How can that be? First of all, Jesus is primarily speaking about grieving over personal sins. But as a secondary meaning grieving over the loss of one's spouse can bring us closer to the Lord than ever before. Romans 5:2-5 sheds light on this thought. "By whom also we have access by faith into this grace wherein we stand, and rejoice in hope of the glory of God. And not only so, but we glory in tribulations also: knowing that tribulation worketh patience; And patience, experience; and experience, hope: And hope maketh not ashamed; because the love of God is shed abroad in our hearts by the Holy Ghost which is given unto us."

Your reaction to your loss can either make or break you. When a loving wife or husband passes into eternity, your reliance on the Lord should become stronger. Never, never be angry with God! You are part of the world that Jesus loves (John 3:16). There is one irrevocable fact that cannot be denied: everyone that is born must sometime die. "And as it is appointed unto men once to die..." (Heb. 9:27). Take this experience to grow in grace and turn your tragedy into a triumph. It certainly is difficult to view such a painful loss into an opportunity to help others. You may feel very weak at this time, but remember this, "And he said unto me, My grace is sufficient for thee: for my strength is made perfect in weakness. Most gladly therefore will I rather glory in my infirmities, that the power of Christ may rest upon me" (2 Cor. 12:9). Paul said, "...when I am weak, then am I strong" (2 Cor.12:10). Ask the Lord Jesus for His strength to carry you through.

To Each His Own When it Comes to Timing

"When will I get back to normal?" "How long will my grief last?" "Is something wrong with me? It's been two years since she/he has been gone. I still have hard times." It is not unusual to have these thoughts. The best advice for you is to allow yourself to fully and completely experience your sorrow.

Some people experience loneliness as never before. Sometimes you may feel lonely when in a crowd. Some feel guilty. "I should have seen it coming." But, don't ever blame yourself. Don't allow yourself to feel guilty. Some go through a time when you feel that you are in a daze. Each person enters this valley differently. Some appear to be "handling things well," but only we who have experienced this know what is going on inside that person's heart. Let me give you some suggestions to help.

- Without a doubt this is the deepest and darkest valley of life. Ask God for courage to face this valley. Remember, He is with you (Psa. 23:4).

- God gave you emotions and feelings. Just as a neglected sore gets worse, so will feelings if they are put off. Allow yourself to feel your feelings. In fact, welcome a quiet time when you can reflect on those "precious memories" and cry all you want. It is healthy and normal to feel sorrow.

- When you feel depressed, cry out to God and read His Word. You have an inner strength that the unsaved do not have. When you are at your weakest point, God's strength can carry you through (2 Cor. 12:9).

What Can I do to Help Myself?

Experience has told me that there are several things you can do to help you go through each day. Here are some suggestions:

◆ Do a lot of praying. God does answer prayers and He cares for you.

◆ Become a close friend with someone who has experienced what you are experiencing.

◆ Make a set time each week for the two of you to go out and eat.

◆ Do something special on the date that your loved one went to be with the Lord. Take the day off. Go to some local tourist attraction. Play some kind of sports: bowling, skating, fishing, etc.

◆ Find things you like to do with your hands.

◆ Write a letter to your departed loved one. Tell him/her how much you love him/her.

◆ Join an e-mail group. Correspond with others.

◆ Buy a present for yourself every so often.

◆ Be sure to do regular exercise. Join a fitness club.

◆ Take a walk each day or use the tread-mill. Remember, looking at a tread-mill does no good.

◆ As you mature and gain strength in the midst of this valley, seek out someone you can help.

◆ Spend holidays with family and friends.

◆ Enjoy life! Don't stay home all the time. Get out and do things.

Attend a support group. Recommend to your church that they start a Precious Memories Support Ministry. There are also support groups run by hospitals and hospice organizations. The Community Hospices of America in Springfield, Missouri were especially helpful to me.

No One Can Know Exactly How You Feel

Your experience is uniquely yours. People may come by with precise formulas to help you through this. Just be kind and listen, but don't heed every advice. They may mean well, but unless they walk in your shoes, they do not know.

There is no "one, two, three" steps that every person who has lost a spouse must experience. Your experience may be entirely different from someone else. The loss of a Mother or Dad, son or daughter, although an earth shattering experience, cannot compare with losing the dearest person you have ever known, your beloved wife or husband. Many of the suggestions and principles in this book may apply to those who have lost other family members, but this book is written by one who has experienced first-hand the "Home-going" of his wife.

Your grief may hold on for two or three years or longer. That is normal and expected. Don't listen to those who may tell you that you have to get on with life. Friends may tell you that they understand, but unless they have walked in your shoes and experienced this deep valley of life, they cannot possibly understand.

Although your friends may sympathize with you, they cannot empathize with you. However, there is One who has suffered as no man has suffered. He has suffered a broken heart and a broken body for you. He not only is the Savior of Salvation, but He loves you and is able to comfort and encourage you as you go through this greatest of all ordeals...and it is truly an ordeal. But with the Great Shepherd by your side, you will be victorious.

You Can't Change What Happened, But You Can Change Your Response

Without a doubt, everything has changed since your life's companion has gone to heaven. All the wishing in the world cannot change what happened, but you do have control as to how you respond. The change is inevitable, but it doesn't have to be a change for the worse. Aldous Huxley, a famous English writer said, "Experience is not what happens to you; it is what you do with what happens to you." You don't have to resign to dismal despair. Some have shut themselves up in their home for months.

The author of this book knows the pain of losing your spouse, but it is a fact that you cannot change what happened. That being the case, you have two choices. You can either give up and resign yourself to a long time of sorrow, grief, discouragement and despair; or, you can, with the help of God, rise above the circumstances and live a life of victory. It is not wrong to enjoy yourself. Once the initial shock wears off, you can lift yourself up and face life with new determination. Determination is what you need. You need not be crushed under the load; you can lift the load and allow the Lord to carry it for you. Remember the scripture? "I can do all things through Christ which strengtheneth me" (Phil. 4:13).

The fact that you are reading this material indicates that you have a desire to overcome. The Prophet Joshua said it well, "...choose you this day whom ye will serve; ..." (Josh. 24:15). You are facing a choice today. Only you can make the choice. No one can do it for you. Accept what has happened. The only way to move beyond the pain is to fully feel it and allow your emotions to move you. With the Lord's help, you can be an overcomer.

Is it Okay to Grieve?

You bet! Following the loss of your spouse, that is the only way to let out your feelings. Man was originally created in the image of God (Gen. 1:26-27). Adam and Eve were created perfect, with no sin. There was no such thing as death. Therefore, we were not created with the ability to handle death. That's why God planted inside each of us the natural ability to grieve. Man and woman were meant to be together. God said that it was not good for man to be alone. When the relationship of husband and wife is severed by the death of one, the result is sorrow. The Bible does not say, "sorrow not," but rather "But I would not have you to be ignorant, brethren, concerning them which are asleep, that ye sorrow not, even as others which have no hope" (1 Th. 4:13). Sorrow, yes! But we don't have to sorrow like those who have no hope. We have a sure Word of hope. "We are confident, I say, and willing rather to be absent from the body, and to be present with the Lord" (2 Cor. 5:8). Now that's something for which to look forward.

Built inside each of us is the hope of eternity and heaven. We would not have that hope of anticipating heaven if there were no heaven. Whereas we grieve and are overcome with sorrow, the prospects of heaven can carry us through and give us the hope that is needed.

Grief should draw us closer to our Lord than ever before. It should also remind us that this life is not all there is and that the sufferings of this life are not to be compared with the glory we shall experience throughout eternity. "For I reckon that the sufferings of this present time are not worthy to be compared with the glory which shall be revealed in us" (Rom. 8:18).

Tears

"What's wrong with me? I suddenly, without warning, break down and cry." Does this describe you? At one Precious Memories Support Ministry luncheon, as I was bringing a devotion, suddenly my voice quivered and a tear came to my eye. A lady who had just lost her husband said, "I didn't know that you men have a hard time like we women." No one is immune to sorrow. Here are some thoughts about tears.

♦ Tears are not a sign of weakness, but of power.

♦ Tears convey feelings more than words.

♦ God answers prayers backed by tears (Isa. 38:5).

♦ Jeremiah, God's prophet, was called "the weeping prophet."

♦ David, called a man after God's own heart, was a man of tears (Psa. 6:6-9). Especially verse 8, " . . . for the LORD hath heard the voice of my weeping."

♦ Tears are a sign of extremely deep love.

♦ God must consider tears to be precious because He evidently stores them in a bottle. " . . . put thou my tears into thy bottle: are they not in thy book?" (Psa. 56:8).

♦ Our bodies were built to react to pain. Sorrow is pain in its fullest state and tears are the natural outcome of sorrow.

♦ Jesus is described in Isa. 53:3 as " . . . a man of sorrows, and acquainted with grief . . ."

In Matthew 11:28, Jesus says, "Come unto me, all ye that labour and are heavy laden, and I will give you rest." No person has experienced grief and sorrow more than Jesus. He knows your sorrow and has promised to give rest to those who come to Him.

Heaven's Splendor! What Encouragement!

[9]And there came unto me one of the seven angels . . . and talked with me, saying, Come hither, I will shew thee the bride, the Lamb's wife. [10]And he carried me away in the spirit to a great and high mountain, and shewed me that great city, the holy Jerusalem, descending out of heaven from God, [11]Having the glory of God: and her light was like unto a stone most precious, even like a jasper stone, clear as crystal; [12]And had a wall great and high, and had twelve gates, and at the gates twelve angels, and names written thereon, which are the names of the twelve tribes of the children of Israel: [13]On the east three gates; on the north three gates; on the south three gates; and on the west three gates. [14]And the wall of the city had twelve foundations, and in them the names of the twelve apostles of the Lamb. [15]And he that talked with me had a golden reed to measure the city, and the gates thereof, and the wall thereof. [16]And the city lieth foursquare, and the length is as large as the breadth: and he measured the city with the reed, twelve thousand furlongs. The length and the breadth and the height of it are equal. [17]And he measured the wall thereof, an hundred and forty and four cubits, according to the measure of a man, that is, of the angel. [18]And the building of the wall of it was of jasper: and the city was pure gold, like unto clear glass. [19]And the foundations of the wall of the city were garnished with all manner of precious stones. The first foundation was jasper; the second, sapphire; the third, a chalcedony; the fourth, an emerald; [20]The fifth, sardonyx; the sixth, sardius; the seventh, chrysolite; the eighth, beryl; the ninth, a topaz; the tenth, a chrysoprasus; the eleventh, a jacinth; the twelfth, an amethyst. [21]And the twelve gates were twelve pearls; every several gate was of one pearl: and the street of the city was pure gold, as it were transparent glass (Rev. 21:9-21).

Wow! What a Place!

Christmas Alone

December was a hard month. My birthday was in December. Also what would have been our 53rd wedding anniversary was in December, just two days before Christmas. Fortunately I was able to visit our children, grandchildren and great-grandchildren. That helped, but the thought kept coming to me that everything was different; I was alone... or... was I really alone? I couldn't feel her warm hand in mine. I knew where she was and how wonderful heaven must be. She was with her Lord and Savior. But in a sense, I felt she was in my heart. So I know what you are experiencing. Here are some things I've learned that help during those "hard days." This comes from experience... and from talking with others.

- ◆ Rely on the Word of God. He is with you at all times. "... for he hath said, I will never leave thee, nor forsake thee" (Heb. 13:5).

- ◆ Think of what a wonderful time he/she is having in heaven. "No eye has seen, no ear has heard, no mind has conceived what God has prepared for those who love him" (1 Cor. 2:9). On the basis of this verse we must admit that heaven's glories, its wonders, its joys, its bliss, are beyond our understanding and imagination.

- ◆ Spend time with family and friends; have a good time. Would he/she want you to be sad during the holidays? Of course not!

- ◆ Attend a Christmas Eve Service at church. If it's hard to sing (I understand that), try to whisper the words.

- ◆ Don't allow yourself to be despondent. This may be very difficult to do, but try to show yourself strong. Remember what the Bible says. "... my strength is made perfect in weakness ... " (2 Cor. 12:9). With the Lord's help, you will overcome.

Accepting What Really Happened

How many times have I asked myself, "Am I living in a dream?" It's just hard to realize that it really happened. Here are some things I think will help you.

- Accept what happened. It is irrevocable! The Bible says, "And as it is appointed unto men once to die . . ." (Heb. 9:27).

- Anticipate the common reactions that can occur. Shock, unbelief, pain, sadness, guilt, confusion and even anger are normal reactions. Some even get angry at God for taking their loved one.

- When you lose your life-long companion, you go through the darkest valley of life. Nothing can compare. Everything changes. If you grieve uncontrollably, don't think there's something wrong with you.

- Mourning is built into us as a way to handle losses. It can be painful and affect you physically. Don't try to put it off. Tears are healthy. Allow yourself to cry. Someday God will wipe away all tears. "And God shall wipe away all tears from their eyes; and there shall be no more death, neither sorrow, nor crying, neither shall there be any more pain . . ." (Rev. 21:4).

- You must tend to your daily needs. Stay active. Find things to do. Drink lots of fluids. Rest and exercise are important at this time. Eat nourishing meals. Call a friend who has experienced the loss of his/her mate and go out to eat with that person.

- Seek help from others. Some grieving is better done in private, but being with others who know from experience what you are going through is important. Hospice groups are available to help. Some hospitals or Funeral Homes offer periodic meetings. The Precious Memories Support Ministry which is usually church-connected is there to help you.

What's He or She Doing In Heaven?

While we grieve on earth, your loved one is in a place beyond our imagination. The Bible tells of one who was caught up into heaven and what he heard. "How that he was caught up into paradise, and heard unspeakable (inexpressible) words (things), which it is not lawful for a man to utter" (2 Cor. 12:4). What your sweetheart is now experiencing is beyond your fondest imagination. They buried the body, but the spirit continues to live. Here are the facts.

● His/her personality continues. In Luke 16, the rich man in Hades had his memory. He pleaded for his 5 brothers (verse 28). Our personality will go on. Do you think you will know less in heaven than you do now? (see 1 John 3:2)

● Your sweetheart continues to love you. Certainly marriage is unknown in heaven (Mat. 22:30), but we will know each other as we are known here on earth. "For now we see through a glass, darkly; but then face to face: now I know in part; but then shall I know even as also I am known" (1 Cor. 13:12). I may not be her husband in heaven, but she knows me as her earthly husband.

● Your sweetheart is busy in heaven. In heaven we will "rest," but that doesn't mean "inactivity." I think she must be in the heavenly choir. God has a job for all those in heaven.

● He/she is like our Savior. Those in heaven will have a body like that of Christ. People recognized Christ after His resurrection. They saw the nail prints. They saw His face and realized it was Jesus. When you get there, you will recognize him/her immediately. As Jesus could walk through closed doors, be in Galilee one second and in Judea the next, those in heaven have that kind of body.

● Your loved one is better by far than ever before. " . . and to be with Christ; which is far better" (Phil. 1:23).

May the Tears of Sorrow Become the Tears of Love, Joy and Anticipation!

I understand that whereas animal love stops when the babies become old enough to care for themselves, human love grows stronger with the passing of years. In fact, it could be said that human love was made for eternity. Think of it this way: did you merely love your departed loved one's physical body or the real person? You see, the real person did not die. He/she merely stepped out of this life and took the next step in heaven. "To be absent from the body is to be present with the Lord." Although my dearest Dixie is not with me now, my love for her continues to grow. I believe we will have a fuller and richer love in heaven than we enjoyed on earth. With that in mind, "May the Tears of Sorrow Become the Tears of Love, Joy and Anticipation!"

Yes, to be sure, the tears of sorrow will flow freely for some time. Tears are natural, healthy and expected. Don't try to hold back your tears. Even Jesus wept at the grave of Lazarus. God made man with the capacity to cry.

Even David cried out, "My tears have been my meat day and night, while they continually say unto me, Where is thy God?" (Psa. 42:3). But later he said, "For thou hast delivered my soul from death, mine eyes from tears, and my feet from falling" (Psa. 116:8). His Tears of Sorrow Became the Tears of Love, Joy and Anticipation.

God wants you to experience this victory. "If ye abide in Me, and My words abide in you, ye shall ask what ye will, and it shall be done unto you" (John 15:7). This is a promise of Jesus and it's for you today. Ask and allow the Lord to make your Tears of Sorrow Become Tears of Love, Joy and Anticipation.

Turning Grief Into Cause

An 80 plus-year-old man looked into the casket of his beloved wife. Being an Alzheimer's patient, he asked, "Is that Eva?" When his daughter said, "Yes, Dad, that's Mom," he quickly bowed his head and under his breath said, "Ohhhh." In three weeks he died. He couldn't take it. He just gave up and died. This happens a lot with the very elderly. But, is that what the loved one in heaven would want? Of course not! The last words Dixie said to me just before the angels took her to heaven were, "Carry on the ministry the Lord gave us!" I said, "Yes, Hon." Well, not only am I carrying on the ministry the Lord gave us to do, but my grief has been turned into cause. The Precious Memories Support Ministry became the cause.

I do not know why Dixie had to go and I'm sure you feel the same way about your loved one. I don't understand, but God isn't through with me yet. Since I didn't go with her, I am certain God has a job for me. That's true of you also. You don't have to stay home all the time and not go out. There are people who could be helped and comforted by your experience. There are things you can do. You don't have to give up and think that you are finished. Let the Lord give you strength. "I can do all things through Christ which strengtheneth me" (Phil. 4:13). "And he said unto me, My grace is sufficient for thee: for my strength is made perfect in weakness. Most gladly therefore will I rather glory in my infirmities, that the power of Christ may rest upon me" (2 Cor. 12:9).

Ask the Lord to turn your grief into a cause and He will do it. He will show you what you can do. You will have a new desire to continue on for Him and for your loved one. Perhaps you now find that you have more time on your hands than ever before. Use it for the LORD! As time passes and you are able, look for ways to encourage others. Go to someone who has just lost their spouse and tell them you understand.

Will We Know Each Other in Heaven?

Dear Reader, can you imagine being in heaven and not knowing even better than we do here on earth? Let me set your mind at ease. Of course we will know each other in heaven. We clearly read in 1 Corinthians 13:12, "For now we see through a glass, darkly; but then face to face: now I know in part; but then shall I know even as also I am known." You will know everything better and you will be known. Even the rich man in hell (Luke 16) did not forget his five brothers and showed concern for them. Do you think those in heaven can possibly forget us? No way!

The Bible makes it clear that there will not be marriage in heaven. "For in the resurrection they neither marry, nor are given in marriage, but are as the angels of God in heaven" (Mat. 22:30). However, heaven will be permeated with love. Without a doubt, your loved one is waiting for you. I dream of walking those golden streets hand in hand with my dear wife. You say, "Where's your scripture for that?" There isn't any and I don't know if that will happen, but I know one thing . . . we will know each other "even as also I am known" now. Marriage is not forever, but love is forever.

So in your time of loneliness, dream on! However wonderful you dream heaven will be . . . just remember, it will be a thousand times more wonderful. "But as it is written, Eye hath not seen, nor ear heard, neither have entered into the heart of man, the things which God hath prepared for them that love him" (1 Cor. 2:9). As you think about heaven, allow your "tears of sorrow to become the tears of love, joy and anticipation." Mark it down! We will not only know each other in heaven, but we will love each other in heaven.

Have All My Friends Forgotten?

It's been two years since the dearest person on earth to me passed away. It's so fresh on my mind. It seems like yesterday, but why don't my friends remember? Where are all those who attended her Coronation Service? It seems like they've all forgotten.

But you will never forget. Losing your life's mate and closest companion is without a doubt the most dramatic and heart-breaking experience that one can experience. Unless he has experienced this valley, he cannot understand what you are going through. I have some suggestions that will help you on your beloved's Home-going anniversary.

- Talk with your family. Sons and daughters may be having a hard time also. They want to help, but unless they know how you are doing, they cannot help you.

- Call up a friend who has lost a spouse. Talking to someone can be a great consolation.

- Take the day off and do something different. Some times you may want someone with you, but at other times, you may want to spend the time alone.

- Call someone who had a part in the funeral service. Perhaps it was a pastor who befriended both of you.

- Pray and thank the Lord for the number of years you had with your spouse.

- Go out to eat with a close friend.

- Visit the grave site. Tell the Lord that you know where he or she is and thank the Lord for his/her salvation.

- Your Bible has a lot to say that can help and comfort you. Read passages such as: John 14:1-3; Revelation 21; Psalm 23; John 11:25-26.

- Attend Church. God's people are always ready to help.

"Encouragement is a Transfer of Strength"

Several people have mentioned to me how that after their dearest friend on earth passed away, they felt like they were living in a dream or in a vacuum. They sometimes say "It just isn't real." They say they feel weak. What they need and you need is a transfer of strength.

"Encouragement is a transfer of strength." Nothing helps like encouragement. You can get encouragement from several places.

First, the Bible has been a source of encouragement for people throughout the centuries of time. "Let not your heart be troubled" (John 14:1). "The LORD is my rock, and my fortress, and my deliverer; my God, my strength, in whom I will trust . . ." (Psa. 18:2). "My help cometh from the LORD, which made heaven and earth" (Psa. 121:2).

Second, the church is a source of encouragement. "Is any sick among you? let him call for the elders of the church; and let them pray over him . . ." (James 5:14). Even Pastors who have not experienced what you are going through don't know how to pray for you unless they are told. God answers prayer, but people need to know the need in order to pray.

Third, there are support ministries such as the Precious Memories Support Ministry that was started to help encourage and comfort people just like you. Seek out a group. Remember, "Encouragement is a transfer of strength." You need encouragement and that's what you can have by being with people who know first-hand what you are experiencing.

"It Does Get Easier"

During the first few weeks when it seemed like the world caved in on me, I was told "It does get easier." At that time I did not understand that. How could it ever get "easier?" But I can attest to the fact that it really does get easier. I believe for most people, the weeks following the funeral are more difficult than the funeral itself. However, in talking with many others as well as my own experience, I strongly advise you not to cut your time of sorrow short. Forget your normal routine for a while. Don't feel like something is wrong with you if your time of grief continues for weeks and months. Take time to remember those "Precious Memories."

Don't be surprised if it seems that in just a few weeks or months after the funeral, you start to have a harder time. The reality of the fact that your loved one is gone gradually sets in. Perhaps when it first happened, you tried to hide your sorrow, but it finally hit you. As I mentioned before, don't try to cut your sorrow time short. Allow yourself adequate time to grieve. It's natural and expected.

In the course of time, it will get easier. This is true of everyone. I cannot tell you how long it will take. Everyone is different. If it seems that you will never "get over it," let me say again, "It does get easier." Time does make a difference. After two years, finally I can look at a picture of Dixie without crying and say, "Hi Dixie, I love you." You may never get to the point when you will never cry or sorrow any more. You may not want to get to that point. I know I don't want to ever get to the point when I don't cry, but I can say once again, "It does get easier!"

The scripture is true when it says, "I can do all things through Christ which strengtheneth me" (Phil. 4:13).

The Pathway of Grief

In talking to a number of people and thinking of my own experience, I find that there are several steps or processes that most all go through when a loved one passes away. Not everyone experiences all of these steps and possibly not in this same sequence. Perhaps knowing in advance what to expect will be a help to you. Sometimes some of these steps may be experienced over again.

Usually first come shock and/or numbness followed by denial. Another word for denial is disbelief. These are some of the common statements made during this time. "This just can't be happening." "I feel like I'm living in a dream." "It just isn't real." The next phase may be anger, but not always. This anger may be directed toward the deceased or even toward God. "Why did you have to go?" "Why did You have to take her now?" God is the last person anyone should be mad at. He dearly loves you and has promised never to leave you. Another feeling that often comes is regret or guilt. "If only I had done more for her when she was living." "There is so much I wanted to tell him but I couldn't bring myself to do it." "If I had only taken her to the doctor sooner." Without a doubt you did all you could. You need not feel guilty. Start thinking of all the wonderful things you did for him. Then may come a feeling of despondency, sometimes called depression. If depression continues for a long time, heart disease can result. Approximately 18.8 million Americans or 9.5% of all adults have depression. This is when help is needed. The answer for these people is God. Some find help by attending a support group such as "Precious Memories" or a hospice group. Remember, God loves you and He wants to help you. Read again Psalm 23. Lastly, resignation to the will of God. This will bring you happiness and the will to keep going.

Should I Attend a Support Group?

There are many support groups out there. Most are just for people who have lost anyone: husband, wife, child, mother, father, etc. Some are just for bereaved parents.

Some funeral homes, hospitals, senior centers and hospices are just a few. A church sponsored Precious Memories Support Ministry is a ministry just for those who have lost a spouse. But you ask, "Should I attend a support group?" Here are some reasons why you should consider attending a support ministry.

♦ Others who have gone down this road can be a big source of help to you.

♦ Listening to others relate their experience and how they are coping with it can encourage you.

♦ Someone might ask the questions you are hesitant to ask.

♦ Others may have the same physical and emotional symptoms that you have and be able to help.

♦ Attendance in a support group will eventually give you strength to open up more.

♦ Sometimes just being with someone who knows first-hand what you are experiencing can help.

♦ In most cases, but not all, the leader(s) of the group is someone who also experienced the loss of his life's mate and can give you the spiritual advice you need.

♦ You may find a special friend in whom you can confide. Calling this person on the phone or going out to eat together can be an uplifting time.

♦ This experience has brought you face to face with the reality of death. If you are not sure of your eternal destination, the leader of this group is there to help you.

♦ Other than perhaps bringing a covered dish, there is usually no charge to attend this meeting.

It Happened So Suddenly!

I called a fellow pastor to let him know I was praying for him. I heard that his wife passed away. I told him about my experience. I took my wife to the doctor because she complained that she couldn't breathe right. The doctor reluctantly ordered an x-ray. After seeing the x-ray, we were told that she had to go the hospital immediately. Following a cat-scan, a cancer doctor showed up in the hospital room. He said, "I'm sorry to have to tell you that you have an advanced stage of cancer and there is nothing we can do." In just seventeen days she was gone. I told that pastor that I only had seventeen days. What he told me was astounding. He said, "I wish I had had seventeen days." "Why? What happened?" I asked. He proceeded to tell me that she was suddenly killed in an automobile accident. I had called to offer him some comfort, but I was speechless for a few seconds.

Here are the thoughts that hit you when this happens. "There are so many things I wish I could have said to her." "If only I had had more time to tell her how much I loved her." "Why did God allow this to happen?" "I just couldn't bring myself to realize she was really dying."

Here's what you need to do about it.

- ◆ Allow family and friends to help.
- ◆ Confide in a close friend who experienced this.
- ◆ After about three months, seek out a support group.
- ◆ Attend church as soon as possible.
- ◆ Take plenty of time to grieve.
- ◆ Never give up on the Lord. He loves you.
- ◆ Find a support group near you and attend when you feel comfortable doing so.

It was Expected! It Happened After a Long Life Illness!

I have often said, "If she had to go, then I'm glad she didn't have to go through months and years of terrible pain." On the other hand, those who witnessed their spouse endure long months of pain might be thankful that they had time to say goodbye. But how many times did the thought come, "God, don't let her/him suffer. Please take her/him home." Some have said they felt guilty thinking such thoughts.

The testimony of many is that it doesn't matter if it was sudden or happened after a long illness; it is still sudden. There is no such thing as getting ready for the eventual death. When it happens, it's just as hard whether it was sudden or not. Here are some things you can do to help yourself following the expected home-going of your spouse.

- Don't blame yourself if you feel guilt for feeling relieved. It is natural that you feel relieved. No one knows what you went through during those long days when you watched your spouse cringe in pain.

- You were already exhausted, but the immediate preparation for the funeral and other final arrangements may be overwhelming. Allow yourself to sit down and rest. Accept help from relatives and friends.

- Your time was all wrapped up in caring for your spouse. Don't feel guilty if you now try to have a good time with your friends.

- Above all, give time for prayer, Bible reading and Church attendance. They know what you have gone through during the months or years of care giving. They have been praying for you. And always remember, the Lord promised never to leave you.

"All Work and No Play Makes Jack A Dull Boy"

Ptahoptep, an Egyptian sage, wrote something similar to the above proverb in 2400 B.C. There is just one problem with that proverb. One element in life is missing. You see life is like a triangle. There are three equal sides and three points of a triangle. They are God, work and play, with God at the top of the triangle.

Following the Home-going of a spouse, the survivor needs to remember that life consists of God, work and play. Work is good, but one should remember to take time to have a good time. Without the Lord's help, a person can never enjoy life to the fullest. God wants you to enjoy life. You may think that you will never enjoy life the way it was; however, you have family and friends. They cannot fill in the void, but gradually you need to; with the help of God, start doing things.

Ask yourself, "What would she/he want me to do?" I cannot imagine your spouse wanting you to sorrow every moment of every day; day in and day out, week in and week out, year in and year out. No, your beloved best friend, lover, life's partner wants you to carry on and enjoy life. Take adequate time to work and play. Above all, don't leave out the most important part of the triangle…God. Life without God is meaningless. Without God, you have no strength. David cried out in 2 Sam. 22:33 "God is my strength and power: And he maketh my way perfect." You may feel weak, but He is strong. The Lord said in 2 Cor. 12:9 " . . . My grace is sufficient for thee: for My strength is made perfect in weakness. Most gladly therefore will I rather glory in my infirmities, that the power of Christ may rest upon me."

"The Hardest Time for Me is When I Am Sick."

How many times have I been told by someone attending our Precious Memories Support Ministry luncheon, "The hardest time for me is when I am sick"? In fact, I have said that also. For some it's those special days like birthdays, anniversaries, the date of his/her departure, Valentine's Day, Thanksgiving, Christmas, etc. The question is, "What can I do to help myself on those days?" When I started this particular article, I thought my fingers would just fly over the keyboard with the answer, but I must admit that there is no certain, easy answer. However, allow me to give you some suggestions.

- Anticipate those days and make plans to do something different.

- Plan to be with family or friends.

- Spend some time alone during that day to dwell on those "Precious Memories."

- Don't hold back the tears. I've been told that bottled-up sorrow without tears could cause other sicknesses to affect one's body. To cry is healthy. Concerning Jesus, we read in Isaiah 53:3 "He is despised and rejected of men; a man of sorrows, and acquainted with grief: . . . " Also we read in John 11:35, "Jesus wept."

- Call up a friend who has experienced what you are experiencing.

- Spend time in prayer. In Matthew 11:28 we read the promise that Jesus will give us rest. "Come unto Me, all ye that labour and are heavy laden, and I will give you rest."

- Always remember, in God's sight, "You're SomeOne Special."®

Not Dead ... Just Sleeping

When Jesus raised the maid back to life after she was dead, Jesus said she was sleeping. Here's what the Bible says. "He said unto them, Give place: for the maid is not dead, but sleepeth. And they laughed him to scorn" (Mat. 9:24). Notice 1 Corinthians 15:51,52, "Behold, I show you a mystery; We shall not all sleep (die), but we shall all be changed. In a moment, in the twinkling of an eye, at the last trump: for the trumpet shall sound, and the dead shall be raised incorruptible, and we shall be changed."

When the Bible says that the dead are sleeping, it is never talking about the soul. The soul goes to be with the Lord at the moment of death. "We are confident, I say, and willing rather to be absent from the body, and to be present with the Lord" (2 Cor. 5:8). The body sleeps until the Lord changes that body to be like His glorious body. "Who shall change our vile body, that it may be fashioned like unto his glorious body, . . ." (Phil. 3:21). Your loved one has merely walked out of his/her natural body and is now in the very presence of the Lord. You see, while we are living on this earth, we really do not see each other; we only see the natural body. The real you is inside your natural body. Your spirit immediately goes to be with the Lord when death comes. That spirit is perfect with no pain or diseases. The day is coming when there will be a great reunion in heaven. We all will receive our glorified, eternal bodies. We will recognize each other and what a day of rejoicing that will be! No wonder the Bible says, "Wherefore comfort one another with these words" (1 Th. 4:18).

When you think of your loved one, lift up your head and take comfort in the fact that your separation is but for a short time compared to eternity.

When Grief is Excessive

There are some people who feel they must continue on sorrowing even when they start to get back to "normal." It is normal and healthy that we shed tears over our loved ones when they are gone, but grief does become excessive when we grieve just to be grieving. I am not a physician, but I have been told by physicians that many of our physical problems are brought on by stress, problems and extreme extended sorrow which in turn results in extreme depression. Some of these diseases are arthritis, meningitis, headaches, uncontrolled vomiting, ulcers, heart-attacks, among other problems. The question you must ask yourself is, "Would my wife/husband who is enjoying the splendor of heaven want me to sorrow as though there is no hope?" Of course not! If after two, three or four years you are still in the deep valley of uncontrolled grief, something is wrong. You need to look up and call upon the God of all comfort to take over your life.

Sorrow, grief and tears are both natural and healthy. Some people even get mad at God for taking their spouse or even mad at their spouse for leaving them. If this is true of you, you need to go to the Lord in prayer and ask Him to help you. Psa. 46:1 tells us "God is our refuge and strength, a very present help in trouble." God can help you through this. Here's another promise of Jesus: "I will not leave you comfortless: I will come to you" (John 14:18). Don't force yourself to grieve. The Bible says that there is "A time to weep, and a time to laugh; a time to mourn, and a time to dance" (Eccl. 3:4). You may feel that you will never get over it. I know you never want to forget. But your loved one in heaven wants you to get on with life and even to enjoy life. The time when you two are together will eventually come.

Coronation Day or Graduation Day

Way back in 1994 I was a guest of a friend who took me to meet Dr. C.S. Lovett, author of 51 plus books. My friend Frank Moseley and I were starting the SOS, Salvation Of Souls ministry, using Morse Code (1837) for a new spiritual use. I mention that because Frank refers to the passing of a loved one as "Coronation Day," while Dr. C.S. Lovett calls it "Graduation Day." I like both of these explanations. Truly it can be said that at the moment of death, we leave these tired, sometimes diseased old bodies for a new one. For that reason, Dr. C.S. Lovett never uses the word "funeral" in his church. I also prefer "Graduation Day" or "Coronation Day."

Perhaps we should readjust our thinking about the things concerning death. No one likes the word "funeral." I like to use either "Coronation Day," or "Graduation Day" when we think of the departure of a loved one who loved the Lord. Just as "there is joy in the presence of the angels of God over one sinner that repenteth" (Luke 15:10), so also must there be a great welcome day in heaven for each one as they enter those pearly gates. What a day of rejoicing it must be in heaven! I think it fitting to call it a "Coronation Day" or a "Graduation Day." With that in mind, there is good reason why we need not sorrow as others which have no hope (1 Th. 4:13).

Hearing your name called, then walking up to the platform to receive your graduation certificate is the thrill of a life-time. But stepping into the splendors of heaven and hearing our Savior say, "Well done, thou good and faithful servant" surpasses anything that earth has to offer.

Talk about shouting . . . well, entrance into heaven and seeing our Lord ought to cause us to shout "hallelujah!"

Should I Remarry?

Now this is not an easy subject to tackle, but for some this is a very important decision. It is very clear according to the Bible that marriage is permissible. "For the woman which hath an husband is bound by the law to her husband so long as he liveth; but if the husband be dead, she is loosed from the law of her husband" (Rom. 7:2). The question however, is "Should I remarry?"

Here are some things to consider:

● Age and length of time you were married.

● What your children think of you marrying again.

● What your children think of the selected person.

● How does this person measure up to your late spouse?

● Do you really know your intended partner?

● Have you both discussed your likes and dislikes?

● Have you had adequate time to grieve?

● How long have you known this person?

● Are you truly in love or are you marrying only because you are lonely and insecure?

● Did you and your past spouse ever discuss what to do in the event of either one dying?

● Have you discussed with your prospective partner things like money, children, where you will live, habits and routines?

● Are you prepared for and willing to change?

● Are both of you of the same faith and willing to attend the same church?

● Is the person you intend to marry saved?

● What are the habits of the person you intend to marry regarding the church?

How do you both measure up to these questions?

What About Suicide?

There is a great misconception that a person who commits suicide goes immediately to Hell. There is only one unpardonable sin, which is recorded in Mark 3:28-29, and it is not suicide. However, suicide is indeed a grievous sin. It is a sin against God and a sin against your loved ones. There have been approximately 6,000 years of human history since the creation. Everyone who has ever lived was here because it was in God's plan. Grief over the loss of their closest friend often makes people feel they can't cope with life any longer. Some of the most spiritual men in the Bible felt this way. Job, for instance, when he lost his family said, "So that my soul chooseth strangling, and death rather than my life. I loathe it; I would not live always: let me alone; for my days are vanity" (Job 7:15-16). Listen to David who was said to be a man after God's own heart, "How long shall I take counsel in my soul, having sorrow in my heart daily? how long shall mine enemy be exalted over me? Consider and hear me, O LORD my God: lighten mine eyes, lest I sleep the sleep of death" (Psalm 13:2-3). These Godly men and others may have wished to die, but they didn't. They turned their grief, sorrow and disappointments over to the Lord and gained the victory. The devil is the only one who would tempt a person to suicide.

If your heart is full of anger, unforgiveness, despair, self-pity, bitterness, vengeance and resentment, will you please right now go to the Lord in prayer and plead with Him to cover you with His love and compassion. Depression is a tool of the devil, but the Lord is more powerful than the devil. Think of your family, friends, church brothers and sisters. Think of how they would feel if you took that horrible step. Remember, "I can do all things through Christ which strengtheneth me."

Suicide and Things to Consider

- Would God want you to override His will for your life? The Bible says, "It is appointed unto men once to die…" Only God knows that time.

- How would your family and friends take this?

- Suicide is self-murder and although murder is forgivable, it is a horrible sin and you will have to give account in the day of judgment.

- How will this affect your relatives and friends?

- Will your insurance cover suicide?

- Have you talked to anyone about this?

- God has given us an instinct to survive. Suicide violates that God-given instinct.

- Jesus said he was *life*; the devil is the father of sin and of *death*.

- Since God can do anything, do you think He cannot give you happiness again?

- God has promised never to leave you or forsake you. He is closer to you now than you think.

- No one knows about tomorrow. God may have something wonderful in store for you. Suicide will destroy all that.

- Contemplation of suicide comes from depression and depression is a tool of the devil. Don't let him get the victory!

- Have you taken this matter to the Lord in prayer?

- Have you talked to your pastor?

- Above all, make sure you are saved, a born again child of God.

- You have a Heavenly Father who loves you and wants to comfort you.

Death is not the end; it's just the beginning. I doubt that it would happen, but if you are asked in heaven about how you died, what would you say?

Part Two

These one-page messages gained from personal experience and from others who have lost a spouse are meant to encourage, strengthen and comfort those who have lost a spouse.

Unless you personally have lost someone extremely close to you, chances are you do not know what to say and not to say or what to do and not do to help others during their time of sorrow. The following pages contain suggestions as to what to say and what to do.

"Encouragement is the transfer of strength."

SOS ™

Things Not to Say

Aman came to me shortly after Dixie passed away and said, "I feel I must say something but I'm afraid to say anything for fear I'll put my foot in my mouth." Many people feel this way so they avoid saying anything. What do you say to comfort someone when you have never passed that way yourself? Sometimes your good intentions have the opposite effect. Before I get into the positive things to say and do, allow me to give my suggestions as to what not to say.

⬧ *"I understand what you are going through."* Do you? Have you experienced the loss of your spouse?

⬧ *"Well, you can be thankful that her sufferings are over."* Yes, that is true, but that doesn't eliminate the sorrow.

⬧ *"Hang in there Mary, the Lord is with you."* Yes, that's right, but that's not what one needs to hear now.

⬧ *"You're handling this well. I am proud of you."* That may be so, but saying that does not help.

⬧ *"God's will is always best."* Yes, that is true, but that's not what needs to be said at this time.

⬧ Even if you have experienced this valley, it is not wise to offer advice based on your experience. Everyone is different. What worked for you may not be what will work for you friend.

⬧ During the first few days or weeks, the survivor is in no frame of mind to listen to or accept words of advice.

About the best I have heard is, "I can't possibly understand what you are going through. I just want you to know that I am here for you. I really do care."

Being specific also helps. For instance, "Would you mind if I brought you over a meal for your dinner tomorrow evening?" Or, "When you are up to it, I'd like to take you out to eat."

Another approach would be, "I can't imagine what you are experiencing. I want you to know I'm here for you. Is there anything I can do for you? I'd be glad to come over and visit you."

More On What Not to Say

For fear of saying the wrong thing, most people fail to say anything. To be sure, if you are close to the person who died, you may find it hard to say anything. Here are some clichés or sentences to avoid.

- ⧫ "Call me if you need anything." Instead, say something specific such as "I would like to help. May I come over and work on your lawn?"

- ⧫ "You've got to stay strong." Sometimes, that is hard and not desired. They may want time to grieve. Everyone handles it differently.

- ⧫ Don't be quick to offer advice or to compare what you went through. Phases like "You ought to . . ." or "You must do . . ." should be avoided.

- ⧫ Don't criticize your friend because you feel he/she is not handling things the way you think they ought.

- ⧫ Avoid saying "Well, she's not suffering any more." That is true, but it does not bring relief during those first few weeks or months.

- ⧫ "You have a lot to be thankful for." That's true, but your friend is not thinking of those things during those hard days.

- ⧫ "We all must go sometime." That's a true statement, but that certainly doesn't help right now.

- ⧫ "God's way is always best." Certainly that is true, but right now your friend doesn't need to be reminded of that.

- ⧫ Don't criticize your friend feel they are not handling themselves as you think they ought.

- ⧫ "You've got to keep busy." Grief takes time and cannot be rushed.

- ⧫ When words fail, give your friend a hug.

- ⧫ "It's been several months you need to get on with life." "You need to..." "You ought to..." "I think you should..." Such suggestions should be avoided. Allow your friend all the time he needs.

Be a Good Listener!

It is better to remain silent and listen than to force your-self to say something that might be taken the wrong way. Some grieving people feel that nobody really understands. There are times when you may feel you must say something. It might be a good idea to say what you want to say out loud when you are not with that person. By doing this, you may realize that it just doesn't sound right and re-word your message.

Each person handles a loss in different ways. You can say one thing to one person and it go over well, but say the same thing to another, and it may not be taken well. For that reason, sometimes "silence is golden."

If you have lost your spouse, then you fully know what your friend is experiencing. When two people who have experienced the same thing get together, very little if anything needs to be said. Sometimes a genuine handshake while looking into each other's eyes is enough. Sometimes a hug will do wonders. From experience I can say that I have received comfort from a hug from a friend. A genuine handshake or a hug along with saying something like, "I'm for you, Joe" or "I'm praying for you. I'm here for you," is all that it takes to render sincere comfort.

Above all, don't feel you must give advice about grieving, even if you have gone through that valley. Everyone is different. Some are extremely emotional and your advice may not be received well. Never tell the bereaved person, "The Lord will help you get over it." It's not something you want to "get over." It's not something to get over. Memories are precious and to be savored. "Precious Memories, how they linger."

Mention the Name of the Deceased

Nothing sounds so pleasant and comforting than for friends to mention the deceased by name. What really means a lot to me is when someone says something like, "I really miss Dixie. I remember the wonderful times we had together." "I know you miss Dixie. I just want you to know I'm praying for you." Saying things like, "I'm sure Dixie must be having a great time in heaven" is much better than "I'm sure she's having a great time in heaven. "

The name of one's departed loved one is precious to the one who remains. It is sad however, that it seems that even some of the closest of friends fail to mention the deceased by name. Why? Some feel that to mention the person by name would trigger some emotional display, so they purposely refrain from mentioning the person by name. Others may find it difficult themselves because they were close to the person. Some may feel that the survivor may not want you to mention his/her name. However, all these reasons are null and void. The one thing the survivor enjoys hearing is the name of their spouse.

When the casket is forever closed, love goes on. For the survivor, the name of the departed loved one is like "music to the ears." It's the spark that keeps one going. It's the name that brings back so many Precious Memories. So when talking to someone who is going through this valley of life, don't just refer to the deceased as "she, he, your wife or your husband," but mention his/her name as much as possible. Next to the wonderful name of Jesus, the name of one's departed loved one is very precious.

Give Your Friend Time to Grieve

There are certainly times when the survivor wants and needs a friend. However, there are other times when he/she needs to be alone. Thinking back and reminiscing is needed. They are probably not ready to resume their normal routine or even attend a support group right away. Don't expect too much out of them.

On the other hand, don't forget them. One thing you can do that will help is to pray. They need God's strength now more than ever before. When you do see him/her, just mention that you are praying for him/her.

In the meanwhile, send a greeting card that contains a good message of comfort. From experience I can tell you that during the first month after a spouse dies, letters and cards of encouragement are received from many friends. However, after the first month, it seems the cards stop coming and the thought hits, "Have they all forgotten?"

Another thing you can do that is very practical is to send a check to your friend. Funeral expenses are astronomical. Unless your friends have good insurance, any help, no matter how small, is greatly appreciated. Usually the Funeral Home will wait one month before charging interest on any unpaid balance. Believe me, those who do send some monetary help will be remembered.

If the person does want to talk, be a good listener. Sometimes knowing what to say is difficult. A sympathetic and understanding listener sometimes can do more good than trying to offer a lot of advice, especially when you haven't passed that way yourself.

I cannot say it enough. Everyone handles grief in a different way. You may be a close friend, but don't be quick to visit your friend or offer advice. Your friend may come to you. That the time to express your love and concern.

What to Say or Do

During the one or two weeks before and following the funeral, cards, letters, thoughtful expressions, flowers, phone calls and offers of help are numerous, but after the friends and relatives are gone, the bereaved wonder where are all their friends. During the funeral and few days or weeks following, the bereaved may be in a daze and the thought hits them, "Is this all a dream?" But the time soon comes when reality hits them and it's then that they need even more help and comfort. Sorry to say, in most cases, they find themselves alone. It's now that they need your help. Here are a few of the hundreds of ways you can help your grieving friend.

♦ Call your friend and say, "I'm going to Wal-Mart and was wondering if I could get you something."

♦ Be a true friend. Be available. Just being there when needed is so beneficial.

♦ "You're sure doing well. You are an inspiration to me." That is much better than "I'm sorry you are having such a hard time with this."

♦ Remember birthdays, anniversaries, Valentine's Day, Christmas and other important days. Call your friend or take him/her out to eat.

♦ Above all, don't avoid seeing your friend. He/she needs you now more than ever.

♦ If the bereaved has children living in the home, offer to watch them while he/she goes shopping or to some other place.

♦ Advise your friends not to make any hasty decisions, such as moving or giving away things. Later they may wish they had those things back.

♦ Suggest they attend a support group such as Precious Memories, or some hospice group.

♦ Listen as your friend shares memories with you.

More on What to Say or Do

Be aware that your friend may be angry. Angry at the doctor, family members, friends and even at God or the person who died. They need assurance. They need to know that God still loves them.

♦ Offer to take him/her to church. Going to church the week after the funeral is not easy, but he/she needs to be with friends.

♦ When they cry, cry with them. Especially if you also were close to the one who died.

♦ Be patient and understanding. Don't expect too much from your fiend.

♦ Tell the bereaved one to write a letter to his/her loved one. It helps to express love this way.

♦ Some bereaved ones feel it helps to keep a diary of their feelings and activities during that first year.

♦ Sometimes just a hug or a squeeze of the hand reassures your friend that you are there.

♦ Nothing beats saying, "I can't imagine what you are experiencing, but I want you to know that I care."

♦ Allow the bereaved people to open up and talk. They may want to talk about their loved ones. Don't interrupt. Be a good listener.

♦ After months or years, when your friend opens up and wants to talk about his/her loved one, listen closely and then mention those happy times you remember.

♦ You might say something like, "I'll be glad to come over and talk with you whenever you want. Just give me a call."

♦ Don't judge your friend's responses. Remember, everyone goes through this valley in their own unique way.

Poems

Every effort has been made to locate the authors of the following poems. Proper recognition has been given to the authors. I appreciate those who granted permission to use their poems.

Miss Me, But Let Me Go

When I come to the end of the road

And the sun has set for me

I want no rites in a gloom filled room

Why cry for a soul set free?

Miss me a little, but not for long

And not with your head bowed low

Remember the love that once we shared

Miss me, but let me go.

For this is a journey we all must take

And each must go alone.

It's all part of the master plan

A step on the road to home.

When you are lonely and sick at heart

Go to the friends we know.

Laugh at all the things we used to do

Miss me, but let me go.

-Author Unknown

Life's Clock

The clock of life is wound but once,

And no man has the power

To tell just where the hands will stop —

At late or early hour.

To lose one's wealth is sad indeed,

To lose one's health is more,

To lose one's soul is such a loss

As no man can restore.

The present only is our own,

Live for Christ with a will;

Place no faith in tomorrow,

For the clock may then be still.

-Robert H. Smith 1932-1982

Do Believe I'll Never Leave You

Do believe I'll never leave you:

Always I'll be in your heart.

Don't forget my soul is near you,

And so we'll never be apart.

-G.P. Palestrina 1526-1594 (?)

Christmas in Heaven

I see the countless Christmas trees around the world below;

With tiny lights like heaven's stars, reflecting on the snow

The sight is so spectacular; please wipe away that tear;

For I am spending Christmas with Jesus Christ this year.

Hear the many Christmas songs that people hold so dear;

But the sounds of music can't compare with the

Christmas Choir up here.

I have no words to tell you, the joy their voices bring;

For it is beyond description, O hear the angels sing.

I know how much you miss me, I see the pain and fear;

But I am spending Christmas with

Jesus Christ this year.

I can't tell you of the splendor or the peace in this place,

Can you just imagine Christmas with our

Savior face to face?

I'll ask Him to lift your spirit as I tell Him of your love;

So then pray for one another, as you

lift your eyes above.

Please let your hearts be joyful and let your spirit sing;

For I'm spending Christmas in heaven

And I'm walking with the King!

Heaven at Last

Angel voices sweetly singing,

Echoes through the blue dome ringing,

News of wondrous gladness bringing...

Ah, 'tis heaven at last!

Now beneath us all the grieving,

All the wounded spirit's heaving,

All the woe of hopes deceiving...

Ah 'tis heaven at last!

Sin for ever left behind us,

Earthly visions cease to blind us,

Fleshly fetters cease to bind us...

Ah, 'tis heaven at last!

On the jasper threshold standing,

Like a pilgrim safely landing

See, the strange bright scene expanding...

Ah 'tis heaven at last!

What a city! what a glory!

Far beyond the brightest story

Of the ages old and hoary...

Ah, 'tis heaven at last!

Softest voices silver pealing,

Freshest fragrances spirit-healing,

Happy hymns around us stealing...

Ah, 'tis heaven at last!

Gone the vanity and folly,

Gone the dark and melancholy,

Come the joyous and the holy...

Ah, 'tis heaven at last!

Not a broken blossom yonder,

Not a link can snap asunder,

Stay'd the tempest, sheathed the thunder...

Ah, 'tis heaven at last!

Not a tear-drop ever falleth,

Not a pleasure ever palleth,

Song to song for ever calleth...

Ah, 'tis heaven at last!

Christ Himself the living splendour,

Christ the sunlight mild and tender;

Praises to the Lamb we render...

Ah, 'tis heaven at last!

Now at length the veil is rended,

Now the pilgrimage is ended,

And the saints their thrones ascended...

Ah, 'tis heaven at last!

Broken death's dread bands that bound us,

Life and victory around us,

Christ the King Himself hath crowned us...

Ah,'tis heaven at last!

—Horatius Bonar 1808-1889

She is Gone

You can shed tears that she is gone

Or you can smile because she has lived.

You can close your eyes and pray that she will come back

Or you can open your eyes and see all that she has left.

Your heart can be empty because you can't see her

Or you can be full of the love that you shared.

You can turn your back on tomorrow and live yesterday

Or you can be happy for tomorrow because of yesterday.

You can remember her and only that she is gone

Or you can cherish her memory and let it live on.

You can cry and close your mind,
be empty and turn your back

Or you can do what she would want: smile,
open your eyes, love and go on.

-Anon

The Garden of Promise

There is a place, I have been told,

Beyond an open gate.

All have been invited

Where friends and loved one wait.

It holds eternal promise

Of everlasting peace,

No pain or sorrow ever comes

And teardrops there have ceased.

Abundant life is evident

Constant, fresh and new,

A garden of provision

With eternity in view.

The promise is awaiting

A place we can abide,

Fulfilled for all who answer

The call to come inside.

—Author Unknown

I Am Now in Heaven

I am now in Heaven—the gates have opened wide,

And now I have the privilege of walking by His side.

The angel choir is singing, and the music is so sweet;

I'll join them just as soon as I have worshipped at His feet.

I am now in Heaven, and the blood-washed throng is here.

I recognize a lot of them—there's not a single tear.

There's joy beyond description and reunions by the score;

There'll be no separations, for we'll be here evermore.

I am now in Heaven—please wipe away your tears!

I've fought the battle, run the race—I'm rid of all my fears.

There is no pain or sorrow here; the heartaches now are past,

I've read and sung of Heaven, and now I'm here at last!

I am now in Heaven, and, oh, the place is grand!

No one could ever tell me all the beauties of this land.

Since I cannot describe it, you'll have to come and see

That it was worth the trials to live here eternally!

-Becky Coxe

Does Jesus Care?

Does Jesus care when my heart is pained
Too deeply for mirth or song;
As the burdens press and the cares distress
And the way grows weary and long?

Does Jesus care when I've said "good-bye"
To the dearest on earth to me,
When my sad heart aches 'till it nearly brakes-
Is it aught to Him, does He care?

Oh yes, He cares; I know He cares,
His heart is touched with my grief;
When the days are weary, the long nights dreary,
I know my Saviour cares.

No Death to the Saint

Where Christ abides, DEATH cannot be.
O grave, where is thy victory?
O DEATH, thou art a conquered foe
To all God's ransomed saints below.

DEATH, to the child of God, means DAWN,
After the long, long night is gone;
Eternal sunshine after the storm
Where sin and Satan cannot harm.

DEATH, to the saint, is but a sleep
Where Angels their sweet vigils keep;
The opening of the garden GATE,
The gate of REST where loved ones wait.

DEATH is but a transportation
By which we reach our destination;
Transports the soul to realms above,
Where all is PEACE and God is Love.

From out this sinful veil of tears
To the raptured GLORY of ETERNAL YEARS,
Forever to behold His FACE
And tell the STORY saved by GRACE.

- Author Unknown -

Appendix
SOS Steps Of Salvation

Although you are honest enough to admit that you do not know the Lord as your Savior, I want you to know that God loves you and He has provided a way for your salvation and a guarantee that Heaven will be your eternal home. At this time when your beloved One has passed away, the God of all comfort knows "You're Some One Special"® and He has heard your SOS cry for help. The following Steps Of Salvation are copied with permission from a 3 X 5 card available on the internet at www.soshelp.com. Here's what you need to know and do.

1st SOS, State Of Sinners
"For all have sinned and come short of the glory of God (Romans 3:23)."

2nd SOS, Sentence Of Sinners
"For the wages of sin is death (Romans 6:23)."

3rd SOS, Source Of Salvation
"For God so loved the world, that He gave His only begotten Son, that whosoever believeth in Him should not perish, but have everlasting life (John 3:16)."

4th SOS, Shortcoming Of Service
"Not by works of righteousness which we have done, but according to His mercy He saved us (Titus 3:5)."

5th SOS, Simplicity Of Salvation
"But as many as received Him, to them gave He power to become the sons of God, even to them that believe on His name (John 1:12)."

"Behold I stand at the door (your heart's door) and knock: if any man hear my voice, and open the door, I will come in to him… (Revelation 3:20)."

Last SOS, Securing Our Salvation

"Dear God, I confess that I am a sinner. I do believe that Jesus Christ died for me to pay my sin debt, and the best I know how, I trust Him and receive Him by faith. In Jesus' Name. Amen."

Special Notice:

This SOS Plan of Salvation on 3" X 5" cards and other soul winning helps are available on the SOS website at www.soshelp.com.

About The Author

From a tract with the title "From Orphan To Christ" that has been printed in both English and Japanese. Over 200,000 of these tracts have been distributed in both the U.S.A. and in Japan.

Dad suddenly disappeared when I was four years old. He was in the U.S. Navy at the time and quite often gambled away his pay. He must have got into a gambling argument and was killed in a fight and thrown overboard. Nobody knows what really happened. When Mother's money ran out, we were forced to leave our fairly comfortable home in Maryland and move from one relative to another, or from one dilapidated house to another. One such house was very interesting to us kids, but I know Mother didn't like it. The house was actually an overpass. We enjoyed seeing the cars and trucks pass under us. This house was condemned by the city and had to be torn down. Wherever I went I had to fight the neighborhood gang boss to see if I could become the new boss. However, I was always afraid to fist-fight and usually came running home with a bloody nose.

Finally my two younger sisters and myself were placed in an orphanage in South Philadelphia. I certainly didn't like the name of that place. It was called "The Southern Home For Destitute Children." By this time I was so bad that my Mother couldn't handle me, so the orphanage was the only answer. Whenever we were caught doing something wrong, we had stiff punishment. At times, because of my meanness, I was forced to stand in the hallway while everyone else slept until one or two a.m., and sometimes, on one foot. But I was clever and devised a spy system to watch out for the workers.

Many times I crawled over the barbed wire wall and was gone for one or two hours without being caught. The thing that caused me more punishment than anything else was my terrible street language. I'll never forget the day I cursed in front of one of the workers. The punishment was horrible. A soft spongy rag was soaked in castor-oil, then poked into my mouth. I was then forced to chew on it for two hours. Every time I moved my mouth, the slimy oil oozed down my throat causing me to choke and almost vomit. But if I did that, then I would have to chew longer, so I just endured it. This horrible treatment just made me rebel and get worse.

Then one night, when I was fifteen, something spectacular happened to me. The orphanage received a phone call from the church across the street. They were having a special meeting and had invited a guest speaker. However, very few of the church members showed up and they were embarrassed because of the empty seats. The idea struck them that if some of the older boys from the orphanage could come just to fill up the seats, the embarrassment would be gone. When asked if we wanted to go I quickly said "yes" because I'd go anywhere just to get away. Then too, it's always better to say "yes" when you know that they'll make you go anyway.

Was I ever surprised when I heard the speaker! What poor English! I doubt that he even completed elementary school. He was just a common Pennsylvania coal miner. His voice was deep and rough, but there was something about him that captured my attention. He spoke as though he cared for me. There was love in his words when he read from the

Bible, "For God so loved the world, that He gave His only begotten son, that whosoever believeth in Him should not perish, but have everlasting life." But I thought that surely He didn't die for me because I was just an insignificant mischievous boy. But then he told us that "Christ Jesus came into the world to save sinners" and I knew that meant me. Then the thought hit me, "How could I ever be saved from my wicked life of sin?" The coal miner read from his Bible, "Believe on the LORD Jesus Christ and thou shalt be saved." I wanted salvation. I wanted everlasting life. I wanted happiness more than anything else. I knew then what I must do. Right there, before he was through speaking, I bowed my head and prayed from my heart, "God be merciful to me a sinner and save me for Christ's sake. Amen!" I opened my heart and received Jesus Christ as my Saviour. Now I knew I had everlasting life, peace in my heart and true happiness. My life changed that very night. There was no more need for the spy system. No more castor oil rags for me! The things I did before, I didn't desire to do again. For the first time I had something for which to live. I knew someone cared for me. At last I had a Father who loved me.

Right after my salvation I felt the Lord leading me to become a missionary. At first, I rejected this call. When my Mother came to see us during visiting hours, I told her that the Lord called me to be a minister. This thrilled her because she was a Christian. However, after graduating from high school I joined the U.S. Air Force. When the Korean War broke out, I was shipped overseas to Japan. I didn't want to

go to any foreign country because I knew the Lord wanted me to be a missionary. I definitely didn't want to meet any missionaries, but God had other plans for me. When I met Missionary Ike Foster, he showed me kindness that no other man had shown me before. He treated me like a father. God worked through him in calling me to Japan. On Christmas Eve of 1950 while riding around the city of Nagoya in an army truck with other soldiers singing Christmas carols, I once again felt the Lord speaking to me. God gave me a great love for the Japanese. One day when Bro. Foster gave the invitation in Chiba, Japan I went to the front of the church and surrendered my life as a missionary to Japan.

You who are reading my story, I would like to say that no matter who you are or what you are, you too, can have this same true peace and happiness and the confidence of eternal life if you will do the following: First, Admit that you are a sinner. God's Word says, "for all have sinned, and come short of the glory of God" (Rom. 3:23). Second, believe that Jesus, God's only son, paid your sin debt when he died in your place on the cross. God's Word says, "For the wages of sin is death; but the gift of God is eternal life through

Jesus Christ our LORD" (Rom: 6:23). Third, accept Him now as your savior. God's Word says, "But as many has received Him (Jesus Christ), to them gave the power to become the sons of God, even to them that believe on His name" (John 1: 12).

If you want this salvation, right now bow your head and

pray the prayer I prayed back on Aug. 15th, 1945: "God, be merciful to me a sinner, and save me for Christ's sake. Amen!" If you'll do this with all your heart, I can guarantee you that you will be saved. Do it now!

Since the writing of this tract, after 25 years in Japan, the author has resigned as a foreign missionary to Japan and has pastored two churches in Missouri. Presently as a Baptist Bible Fellowship Missionary, he has a weekly Japanese Church service in Springfield, Missouri. In addition to this ministry, he has started the Precious Memories Support Ministry with the purpose of rendering help, encouragement and comfort to those who have lost a spouse. He has also been involved in the SOS Soulwinning Ministry since 1992. 3" X 5" cards with the SOS Plan of Salvation and other helps are available at the SOS web site at www.soshelp.com.

-Recommended Websites-

The Author's Website
http://www.billhathawayministries.org/

The SOS Soul Winning Ministry
http://www.soshelp.com/

Baptist Bible Fellowship International
http://www.bbfimissions.com/bbfidnn/

Baptist Temple, Springfield, MO
http://www.baptisttemple.net/

Friendship Baptist Church, Wichita, KS
http://www.friendshipbaptistofwichita.com/

Northside Baptist Temple, Mt. Vernon, MO
http://fp1.centurytel.net/NorthsideBaptist/

Ray Melugin, Evangelist
http://www.raymelugin.org/

Bryant Ministries
Southern Gospel Music
http://www.bryantministries.com/

Wilson Creek Baptist Church
http://www.wilsoncreekbaptistchurch.com/

Japan Baptist Bible Fellowship
http://www.jbbf.org/

Integrity Home Care
http://www.integrityhc.com/

R. L. Hymers Jr.

Website for Japanese Sermons
http://www.rlhymersjr.com/

Community Hospices of America
http://www.chahospice.com/

Web Designer Chris Jaquess
http://www.twotalldesign.com/

How to Start and Operate a Precious Memories Support Ministry

When my dear wife Dixie was diagnosed as having an extremely fast moving cancer, I called my friend who is the owner of Integrity Home Care. He immediately sent his very qualified and caring nurses and aides to help care for her. They were a great help and comfort to us. However, it became obvious to them that, for us, the Community Hospices of America in Springfield, Missouri should take over. They, too, were very caring and were able to give the comfort and care Dixie needed. The Hospices people invited me to a six-week support group. I received much support and comfort from these weekly sessions with others who had gone through this deepest valley of life. Many call the hospices nurses and staff "angels" and rightly so.

Through this experience I realized that there ought to be a church-centered support group for those who have lost a spouse. Thus the Precious Memories Support Ministry was started. They say "experience is the best teacher." That is certainly so. With the suggestion of the publisher, I am adding this appendix to the second printing with instructions and suggestions as to How To Start and Operate a Precious Memories Support Ministry. These are only suggestions from experience and may have to be adapted to the circumstances of each church. It is my desire that each church keep the name "Precious Memories Support Ministry." This ministry has brought me from the valley to the mountaintop. In my mind, it was started in honor and in memory of the dearest person in the world to me, my wife Dixie. However, your group or chapter of Precious Memories Support Ministry could be in honor or in memory of your own dear wife or husband. Here are my suggestions and plan.

1.   The Need

Almost any church of any size and of any denomination has a need to start a support ministry for those who have lost a spouse. If the need does not exist now, it will. Every church, every family, every individual has either directly or indirectly experienced the eternal departure of a loved one. The Bible says, "It is appointed unto men once to die… (Heb. 9:27)." Tears, grief and sorrow are a natural outcome of this valley of life. Therefore, the need is great.

2.   Where To Meet

Without a doubt, the best place to meet is in the local church. This ministry ought to be sponsored by the church as an out-reach of the church. The church members need to bathe this ministry in prayer. People are hurting and need the comfort that the Precious Memories Support Ministry can give. Most churches have a fellowship hall or some kind of dining room. This would be the best place to meet.

As a second choice for a place to meet, I recommend some Senior Center located close to the sponsoring church. Most cities have a Senior Center that is available and is usually free. There are usually many people who attend the Senior Centers who have gone or are now going through this valley and would like to attend. In any event, a local church should be the sponsor. This is not only an opportunity to render help and comfort to those in need, but as an outreach of the church, it is an opportunity to invite people to the church.

3.   When to meet

Meeting once each month seems to work in most places. You can decide on a certain Saturday each month such as the second Saturday, or whichever day works best for your situation. Do everything possible not to change this time unless there is an extreme, unavoidable emergency.

4. Practical things needed

◆ A colorful brochure. This brochure should contain information as to the time, dates and place of the meetings. A full schedule of services for the sponsoring church should be included. A picture of the person(s) in charge and his or her description would be important. Scriptures about death and comfort would be fitting. The following scriptures are only suggestions: Matthew 10:28, 1 Thessalonians 5:23, 2 Corinthians 5:6-9, Philippians 1:22-24, Job 19:25-27, 1 Corinthians 15:21-22, John 14:18, 2 Corinthians 1:4. In the brochure, perhaps a nice poem or song that touches the heart should be included. The song "Precious Memories" might be a good one to include.

◆ Display signs. A sign showing the entrance to the meeting should be displayed outside the door where the meeting is held. Any sign company can make a professional looking sign that can be inserted in the ground by the entrance door.

◆ Business cards. The person(s) in charge should have business cards made for distribution. They might contain a picture of the one in charge, church address, date and times of meetings and any other information necessary.

◆ Magazines and booklets. Any Hospice organization would be willing to give you magazines and other booklets that you can have available at the meetings. This book, *No More Tears*, ought to be available for purchase. Many report that they have received comfort from the reading of this book.

How to Conduct the Meeting

- Decide if your meeting is to be a luncheon or a coffee, juice, donuts and cookie time.

- If a luncheon, you might ask the people to bring a potluck dinner.

- If a social time with coffee and juice, perhaps the church could provide the drinks and donuts.

- It is a good idea to have a nametag for each person to wear.

- A card should be given to each person to fill out with the following: name, address, phone number, name of departed loved one and date of his/her birth, death and birthday.

- While people are bringing in food, have chairs prepared for them to sit and chat with each other.

- After most of the people are finished eating, give your own testimony of how you are coping with your loss and urge those who wish to do so, to give their testimony. This is an important part of the meeting, because hearing the experiences of others encourages those just going through this valley.

- Talking about their loved one should be encouraged. Most friends at church don't know what to say and even avoid mentioning the name of the departed loved one.

- A short devotion should be given that is geared to encourage and comfort.

- Always announce when the next meeting will be held.

- Make an announcement that the leader(s) will remain behind after all have gone in order to speak personally with any who desire such a meeting.

- Occasionally, it would be good to take the group to the

lake, park or to some musical show. The grieving person needs to know that he or she is not betraying the love for the departed one, and that it truly is acceptable to be happy in the midst of the grief.

♦ As a suggestion, try not to have more than 20 to 25 in a group. If the need exists, think about starting another group at a different time.

♦ The best leader for this ministry would be a pastor or retired minister whose wife is already in heaven. If no one is available, the pastor of the host church could do this until someone who has gone through this experience is available.

♦ A radio announcement of church and civic news, which is normally free, should be considered.

♦ The local newspaper would be willing to carry a story about this ministry.

♦ This is extremely important, and the secret of success for the meetings depends on this: Find someone who has a genuine burden for this ministry who will keep records of the attendees and will call them the day before the meetings.

♦ Take pictures of the meetings and have them included in the church's web site.

♦ Make sure the upcoming meeting is announced from the pulpit and included in the weekly church bulletin.

♦ These suggestions should be adapted to each situation.

Sample Devotion Outlines

The Loneliness of Sorrows

The most difficult kind of sorrow is the Loneliness of Sorrow. No one knows this except those who have experienced it. I guess the most used remark I get is "I can't imagine." Or "I've never experienced it and hope I never will." Or "I don't think I could handle it" (1 Thess. 4:13). "But I would not have you to be ignorant, brethren, concerning them which are asleep, that ye sorrow not, even as others which have no hope." It is not wrong to sorrow...it is wrong to sorrow "as others who have no hope." I want to bring you a few thoughts of encouragement today.

God Loves You

Some think that if God loves you, you shouldn't get sick, but Lazarus got sick... and died. Perhaps Mary and Martha might have questioned the love of the Lord Jesus. Lazarus certainly must have been walking in the will of God, but still got sick. But God still loves you!

⬥ Love & Suffering. Suffering is not incompatible with love. Sometimes we ask for our problems or sickness. It's our own fault. If God intervened every time we were heading for a calamity, this world would really be a mess. The cross is proof that suffering is not incompatible with love.

⬥ Love & Delays. Mary and Martha might have questioned God's love because of our Lord's delay. John 11:6 "When he had heard therefore that he was sick, he abode two days still in the same place where he was." Jesus didn't hurry... He didn't have to.

⬥ Love & Disappointment. The Sisters were disappointed. Listen to Mary. "Then when Mary was come where Jesus was, and saw him, she fell down at his feet, saying unto him, Lord, if thou hadst been here, my brother had not died" (John 11:32). There is no need to question God.

85

♦ Love & God's Word. How do we know that God loves us? Because the Word of God tells us so. Never judge the love of God by your feelings or your circumstances! In fact, in Mary & Martha's case, the neighbors noticed that Jesus loved them before they did. "Then said the Jews, Behold how he loved him" (John 11:36)!

Christ is with You

The second assurance is Christ is WITH YOU. We have an advantage that Mary & Martha did not have. Jesus had to come to Bethany. He was limited to His physical body then. But now He is ALWAYS with us. "Let your conversation be without covetousness; and be content with such things as ye have: for he hath said, I will never leave thee, nor forsake thee" (Heb. 13:5).

♦ He Knows Your Sorrow. "Thou tellest my wanderings: put thou my tears into thy bottle: are they not in thy book" (Ps. 56:8)? The suggestion here is that God keeps a record of your tears.

♦ He Shares Your Sorrow. He not only KNOWS your sorrow, but He SHARES your sorrow. "Jesus wept" (John 11:35). Isaiah 53:3 says He is a man of sorrows, and acquainted with grief.

♦ He Can Transform Your Sorrow. He KNOWS your sorrow. He SHARES your sorrow. He can TRANSFORM your sorrow. He said to Martha, "I am the resurrection, and the life; he that believeth in me, though he were dead, yet shall he live. And whosoever liveth and believeth in me shall never die" (John 11:25,26). Death for the believer is only sleep. Jesus said in verse 11, "Our friend Lazarus sleepeth." The body sleeps in the grave; the spirit goes Home to be with the Lord.

God's Will is Best

Assurance number 1 is that GOD LOVES YOU. Assurance number 2 is that CHRIST IS WITH YOU. Assurance number 3 is GOD'S WILL IS BEST.

⬧ God Has His Time. The disciples couldn't understand why Jesus waited two days. Jesus said, "Are there not twelve hours in the day" (John 11:9). He has a divine time schedule.

⬧ God Has His Purposes. One purpose was to strengthen the people involved. Jesus said "And I am glad for your sakes that I was not there, to the intent ye may believe" (John 11:15). The faith of the disciples was increased by this experience.

⬧ I Don't Know God's Purposes In What You Are Going Through. It is not mine to question. From past experiences, I know God's way is always the best way... even though I don't understand.

God Will be Glorified if You Believe

⬧ The Glory of God is the Most Important Thing In The Universe. You say, "But that's a difficult experience for people to go through just for the glory of God." It was difficult for Jesus to die on the cross for the glory of God, but He did it -- and He did it for you!

⬧ He Will Be Glorified Through Your Testimony.

⬧ He Will Be Glorified Through Your Life.

God loves you! Christ is with you! God's will is best! God will be glorified if you believe!

God's Gift to His Grieving Children

God has a message in His Word for every human need. God has not left us in the dark about things that matter to them. God loves us and does not want us to be ignorant of those truths that would give us hope and comfort in troubling times. There is nothing more troubling and mysterious than death. We cannot see beyond this world. We cannot see the angels as they carry the souls of our saved loved ones to Heaven to be with the Lord. We cannot see them take that first step into Glory. We cannot see their faces when they first see their Savior. We cannot see their Heavenly Home. Oh, how we wish we could get just a glimpse of Heaven... a glimpse of our loved one. What is she (he) doing right now? Can I get a message to her (him)? Does she (he) see me? I doubt this, but the thoughts are still there. Sometimes these thoughts are so overwhelming that in my case, I break down and cry. I can't help it. But the sunshine of God's love shines through to calm our spirits and heal our broken hearts. Notice the Scripture reading:

> [13]But I would not have you to be ignorant, brethren, concerning them which are asleep, that ye sorrow not, even as others which have no hope. [14]For if we believe that Jesus died and rose again, even so them also which sleep in Jesus will God bring with him. [15]For this we say unto you by the word of the Lord, that we which are alive and remain unto the coming of the Lord shall not prevent them which are asleep. [16]For the Lord himself shall descend from heaven with a shout, with the voice of the archangel, and with the trump of God: and the dead in Christ shall rise first:[17] Then we which are alive and remain shall be caught up together with them in the clouds, to meet the Lord in the air: and so shall we ever be with the Lord. [18]Wherefore comfort one another with these words (1 Thess. 4:13-18).

God Reveals the Secret

🔹 "But I would not have you to be ignorant…" (I Thess. 4:13a). Jesus does not want his followers to be unaware of their loved one's condition. Therefore He takes us beyond the veil and assures us of their comfort.

🔹 Christ told us of the poor beggar and how after he died he was carried by the angels to be comforted.

The Scriptures tell us that, for the Christian, "to be absent from the body is to be present with the Lord." God tells us the secret. He lets us know what is on the other side of death. He tells us of that which our human eyes cannot see.

God Reduces the Sorrow

🔹 "…that ye sorrow not, even as others which have no hope" (1 Thess. 4:13b). He doesn't REMOVE the sorrow for we are still going to grieve over being separated from our loved ones. To have no hope is tragic, but that is not our case. We have the assurance of God that we shall see our departed loved ones again.

🔹 Christ understands our grief. "For we have not an high priest which cannot be touched with the feeling of our infirmities; but was in all points tempted like as we are, yet without sin" (Heb 4:15).

🔹 Christ wept at his friend Lazarus' tomb.

[33]When Jesus therefore saw her weeping, and the Jews also weeping which came with her, he groaned in the spirit, and was troubled, [34]And said, Where have ye laid him? They said unto him, Lord, come and see. [35]Jesus wept. [36]Then said the Jews, Behold how he loved him! [37]And some of them said, Could not this man, which opened the eyes of the blind, have caused that even this man should not have died (John 11:33-37)?

God Refers Us to the Savior

⬧ "For if we believe that Jesus died and rose again, even so them also which sleep in Jesus will God bring with him" (1 Thess. 4:14). Jesus conquered the grave and if we are "in Him," we are made victorious over death as well.

⬧ When we hurt, it is always good to remember our Savior. Think about the fact that our loved one is right now with Him. To be with Jesus... what consolation! What comfort!

God Recites the Schedule

⬧ "[15]For this we say unto you by the word of the Lord, that we which are alive and remain unto the coming of the Lord shall not prevent them which are asleep. [16]For the Lord himself shall descend from heaven with a shout, with the dead in Christ shall rise first: [17]Then we which are alive and remain shall be caught up together with them in the clouds, to meet the Lord in the air: and so shall we ever be with the Lord." (1 Thess. 4:15-17).

⬧ The living have no advantage over those whose bodies are asleep in Jesus. In fact, they will be resurrected first. Then in an instant, we will join them on the way up. Hallelujah!

God Reminds Us to Give Solace

⬧ "Wherefore comfort one another with these words" (1 Thess. 4:18).

⬧ He gave us His Word so we could comfort each other with it. He wants us to comfort others who are going through the valley we are experiencing.

⬧ Without the Lord, there is no hope! With the Lord, there is positive hope! Although we grieve and sorrow, that sorrow is lessened with the knowledge that our loved ones are in a wonderful place, comforted, loved, happy and waiting for us.

Thank God every day that you are saved and that your loved one is saved and in the very presence of his (her) Savior. What a wonderful reunion we will have. I'm looking forward to that great day. In the meantime, we've got a job to do. Let's keep busy doing the Lord's work.